The LeBaron Russell Briggs Prize
Honors Essays in English . 1969

MELVILLE'S *ISRAEL POTTER*
Reflections on the American Dream

MELVILLE'S *ISRAEL POTTER*

Reflections on the American Dream

Alexander Keyssar

Harvard University Press

Cambridge, Massachusetts

1969

FOR MY PARENTS

CONTENTS

Introduction—1

1. Patterns and Causes—11
2. Comedy and Pathos—37
3. The Truth of the Tale—43

Works Consulted—54

Notes—55

MELVILLE'S *ISRAEL POTTER*

Intrepid, unprincipled, reckless, predatory, with boundless ambition, civilized in externals but a savage at heart, America is, or may yet be, the Paul Jones of nations.

"To what end do you lead that man about?"

"To no end in the world, sir. I keep leading him about because he has no final destination."

—*Israel Potter*

INTRODUCTION

It is, perhaps, a more than accidental irony that Melville's *Israel Potter: His Fifty Years of Exile*, ostensibly a tribute to a forgotten hero of the American Revolution, has suffered the same fate as its leading character: neglect and virtual oblivion. The book was published, in serial form, well after Melville's contemporary popularity had begun to wane, and in modern criticism it has been relegated to the unfortunate status of a minor work by an author who also produced Major Work.[1] To be sure, *Israel Potter* hardly bears comparison with *Moby Dick*, nor can the poor private of Bunker Hill stand up to the heroic Ahab. Yet Melville was conscious of the difficulties inherent in making his subject a popular one. He knew well "that to the craped palace of the king lying in state, thousands of starers shall throng, but few feel enticed to the shanty" of the pauper.[2] If Melville's purpose in writing *Israel Potter* was to entice more readers and critics to the shanty, to lead the public to an awareness and contemplation of a particularly dismal and forgotten type of human fate, then the neglect that the book has received may be either a token of his failure or an ironic vindication of his aim.

Clearly, any study of *Isreal Potter* must consider the book in the context of Melville's other writing during the period 1853–1856. Beginning with "Bartleby the Scrivener" and ending with *The Confidence Man*, this period presents a body of work that is markedly distinct from *Moby Dick* and *Pierre*. Throughout these years, Melville displays an interest in the common man rather than the elevated hero. He is concerned with conventional rather than extraordinary human problems. He focuses upon those elements of human life which are obstacles to the felicity of masses of men: failure, poverty, loneliness, and the defeat of hopes and expectations.[3] This change of thematic emphasis, of course, is accompanied by a shift in rhetoric from the exaltation of *Moby Dick* to the almost total irony of *The Confidence Man*.

It has become a commonplace of criticism to attribute these alterations in Melville's work to some form of that disease known as "creative exhaustion." For instance, Newton Arvin, in his study of Melville, criticizes *The Confidence Man* on the grounds that the "swindles are simply not swindles on a grand scale." "What had happened to Melville," he asks, "that he could not imagine chicaneries more imposing than these?" Arvin concludes, with a note of wistfulness, that Melville "had lost his sense of the tragic."[4] There are tricky assumptions lurking behind criticism of this type. Foremost is the tacit assumption that the movement from high tragedy to low mimetic or domestic tragedy[5] represents a decline in artistic value, and that such a decline could only be the product of failing creativity. Without wishing to engage in a dispute about what constitutes great art, I would like to point out that Melville's change of subjects *may* have resulted from personal and creative exhaustion, but it may also have been the product of conscious choice. In particular, if *Pierre* does represent, in part, a deliberately defiant statement to a certain school of literary standards[6] and if, as has been claimed,[7] Melville made fewer concessions to popular taste from 1853 to 1856 than at any other time during his career, then the tone and themes of that body of work may well be attributed to artistic and intellectual integrity rather than to sheer enervation.

Why Melville wrote what he wrote is, of course, ultimately his secret. Criticism has a more objective role, and for the student of Melville, part of that role consists in resisting the temptation to denigrate irony and pathos because they are not tragedy, to denigrate *Israel Potter* because it is not *Moby Dick*. Let us try then, in examining *Israel Potter*, to focus sympathetically on this "plebian Lear" (p. 230) and give him his due independent of the merits of his more majestic predecessors.

Israel Potter is not an easy book to decipher. There is

no handy critical template that, when applied to the text, will reveal the meaning and method of the book. Melville's eighth long work of fiction, which first appeared in nine installments in *Putnam's Monthly Magazine*, is a strange combination of history and allegory, picaresque adventure and ironic symbolism. As source books, Melville used Ethan Allen's autobiography, a biography of John Paul Jones (whom Melville called simply Paul Jones), Nathaniel Fanning's *Narrative of the Adventures of an American Naval Officer*, and, naturally, the *Life and Remarkable Adventures of Israel R. Potter*, which he had obtained by chance in 1849.[8] Although Melville relied quite heavily upon his sources,[9] the work is not simply a rehashed potboiler; nor, after a careful reading, could one support the claim that *Israel Potter* is "hardly more than a heap of sketches" for a masterwork that was never written.[10] A complete and meticulous examination of Melville's text is a subject for a longer study than the present one; nevertheless, within these pages, I shall try to outline those themes and techniques which reveal the internal coherence of *Israel Potter* and which provide insights into Melville's intellectual and literary concerns during the crucial years shortly before he brought an end to his career as a professional writer of fiction.

One may begin by simply reflecting upon the more

evident thematic issues of *Israel Potter*. The foremost of these is the fact that human hopes and expectations are, with notable frequency, simply not realized in the world of Israel Potter. This theme is continually expressed by the patterns of action of Potter's adventures. It occurs both in small details (for example, Israel expects to be served wine and pastry by Benjamin Franklin, but he is not) and in large, sweeping movements (for instance, he expects certain rewards from life in return for his dedicated and courageous actions, but none are forthcoming). In a sense, this is Melville's version of a conflict which later thinkers would call the "absurd": a conflict between man's hopes and desires for happiness and the conditions of the actual world that prohibit happiness. In Melville, of course, this theme is not found only in *Israel Potter*. Throughout his work, one finds individual men seeking either to overcome or to cope with the fact that their sojourn on earth is not as pleasant as it might have been. *Pierre*, "Bartleby," "Cock a Doodle Doo," and "Jimmy Rose" offer ready examples of this situation, and *Redburn* presents an even more crucial experience. Redburn's adventures, above all else, depict the growth of existential disillusionment:[11] a boy, filled with hopes about the possibilities of happiness, gradually experiences the world and, as he does so, is slowly alienated from his prior expectations. Nor can one forget that this same young boy, through worldly experience, has become the resigned narrator who notes that "the silent reminiscence of hardships departed is sweeter than the presence of delight."[12] For Melville, the process of human growth is an awakening to the limitations of earthly existence. Paradise has been lost: "imperishable bliss," as Wallace Stevens termed it in "Sunday Morning," is not man's destiny.

The controlling theme of *Israel Potter*, then, is summarized by Israel's gloomy premonition "that being of this race, felicity could never be his lot" (p. 228). Yet it is clear that in *Israel Potter*, as in *Pierre* and many of the short stories, the obstacles to felicity are often social or socioeconomic. Poverty, violence, and inhumane working conditions frequently prevent Melville's characters from realizing their hopes. Society has somehow failed many of its members. As Pierre learns, or perhaps fails to learn, man can exist only in society, and his happiness is contingent upon social conditions. Since, given these premises, the history of civilization may be viewed as the record of man's actions and schemes in search of social felicity, Melville's treatment of social evils suggests an entire reappraisal, on his part, of the value of civilization. This notion is made explicit at the end of Chapter 19 of

Israel Potter when Melville writes: "What separates the enlightened man from the savage? Is civilization a thing distinct, or is it an advanced stage of barbarism?" (p. 186). What good is civilization if civilized man is not happy? And what is wrong with civilization that its members cannot attain felicity?[13]

These ideas relate, both in the abstract and in *Israel Potter*, to America and to democracy. If men could find happiness only in a perfectly just society, then it was of great importance that such a society come into being. And where else but America could this happen? America, free from the thralldom and evils of European society, would eliminate suffering and injustice. America, the home of freedom and opportunity for the common man! Or so, at least, ran the political and literary rhetoric of Melville's time,[14] a rhetoric which led in *White Jacket* to Melville's proclamation that "we Americans are the peculiar, chosen people—the Israel of our time; we bear the ark of the liberties of the world."[15] This quotation is ironic in light of *Israel Potter*, and the irony is revealing. Melville had long been irritated by chauvinistic rhetoric,[16] and, as F. O. Matthiessen wisely points out, there was a serious split between Melville's belief in the potential good of American democracy and his observations of the evils extant in that society.[17] Poverty, slavery, war, and

7

assembly-line industrialization were all blemishes upon the optimistic promise of America. This promise, or expectation, was simply that America would be the ideal society, the society in which men's dreams would be fulfilled and their hopes attained.

At this point, one begins to see the imaginative origins of *Israel Potter*. One begins to see why the little pamphlet printed "on sleazy gray paper" (p. v) and entitled *Life and Remarkable Adventures of Israel R. Potter* so arrested Melville's attention. The promise of American democracy is, or at least can be seen as, the collective expression of each man's desire for happiness, for the promised land. The promise of America is then fused with the existential promise of human life itself: that man, on earth, will find happiness. The myth of America becomes the belief that happiness exists. And the reality of America becomes the social symbol that human expectations are indeed defeated. Israel Potter fights for the creation of America and spends the rest of his life unsuccessfully trying to cash in on America's promise. Why he is unsuccessful is the subject of Melville's book. The reason is not simply that he was forced to live in England: it is no accident that Melville consciously and consistently toned down the pro-American and anti-English passages from Potter's own narrative. For Melville, the cause of Israel Potter's failure can be found only by a long, careful, and often painful scrutiny of America, of civilization, and of that peculiar creature, man himself.

It is in this ideological context, then, that one must look at both the details and the overall narrative of *Israel Potter*. It is the story of a courageous, common, virtually faceless man who struggles, without reward, against the obstacles to his happiness; a man who, above all, wishes to return to America, and in whose mind felicity and America are equated. He is an American and has led a life of extraordinary adventure. Yet, because he is faceless and because of the symbolic rendering of his story, he becomes Melville's poor Everyman. His hopes and his fate display a significant lack of congruence. For Melville in 1854, faced with a failing career, financial worries, a tormented mind, and a strife-torn America, the story did indeed become, as William Ellery Sedgwick notes, "an image of his own soul."[18] Yet Sedgwick does not go far enough: *Israel Potter* expresses not simply Melville's personal dilemma, but rather the elements of that dilemma which Melville conceived to be widespread, if not universal. Tragedy had become all too real to Melville:[19] not the grand tragedy of Lear or Ahab, but the simple tragic fact of men, on earth, confronted by obstacles that they could not overcome.

Israel Potter, like many of Melville's works, is a story of failure. It derived from a documented account of a real man's sufferings and misadventures. In Melville's hands it became an exploration of the patterns and causes of man's fate. The nature of that exploration, as it is expressed in narrative and symbolic fiction, is the subject of the following chapter.

The many episodes and sketches that constitute the materials of *Israel Potter* are made to cohere, ostensibly, by the device of biography. The book is, or at least appears to be, the story of Israel Potter's life: it begins with his birth, ends with his death, and treats, with varying emphasis, those actions and adventures which befell him during the period between his "two eternities." Israel himself is almost always on stage, and other characters are introduced and largely discussed only as they cross the path of the hero. Yet many of the episodes and descriptions in *Israel Potter* contribute little, if anything at all, to a knowledge of the narrative life history of the leading character. The long chapters on Benjamin Franklin and Paul Jones are obvious examples. Moreover, Melville, as a biographer, pays pitifully little attention to the thoughts and psychology of his subject. Perhaps, then, as Leon Howard has suggested, the story of Israel Potter is merely a mechanism through which Melville can present his historical sketches.[20] This possibility is in part refuted by the ideas presented in the Introduction and, by the end of this chapter, it will, I hope, be seen to be untenable.

There are, thus, two basic types of materials in *Israel Potter*. One consists of the basic story of Israel's life: a great deal of the text serves simply to inform the reader, in a general survey, about the sequence and circumstances of Potter's adventures and misadventures. These narrative portions of *Israel Potter* do, however, also contain motifs, or repeated patterns, that possess symbolic as well as literal meaning.

The second type of material is composed of those sections of the text which, for a variety of reasons, are not fundamental elements of the narrative surface of the book. The emphasis of these scenes is not on Israel's life. They illumine nothing about the specific causal and sequential relations that lead to the specific destiny of Israel Potter: they do not have a narrative coherence in the book. They do, however, have a symbolic coherence. For this reason, the most revealing way of approaching the text of *Israel Potter* is to view the "story" or plot as an exemplum punctuated by symbolic episodes that function as commentary upon the exemplum. If, as I have maintained, the book is in some sense a story of the universal common man, then the plot can be seen as a simple fable of the common man's fate and the interpolated episodes and sketches as paradigms and explanations of that fate. Each "interpolation" has a precise relation to the fable of Israel Potter, and, taken together, these episodes provide significant insights into Melville's view and explanation of man's defeated expectations.

The two types of structural symbols—narrative motifs and the interpolated scenes and sketches—are not always clearly distinguishable from each other, but such a generic distinction is not crucial to this study.[21] For the sake of clarity, I will consider the specifically American or historical passages separately from those passages which have a more "existential" meaning. An understanding of *Israel Potter* is contingent upon a careful determination of the symbolic content of these portions of the text.

Of primary importance is the narrative and symbolic origin of Israel's career as a wandering exile from the promised land. Man's failure to achieve earthly happiness is an age-old literary theme. Its connection with the expulsion of Adam and Eve from the garden of Eden is obvious, and it is a significant, if heretofore unrecognized, fact that Melville, in *Israel Potter*, makes considerable use of the archetype of the garden. The first mention of a garden is in the third chapter, when Israel is trying to escape from two inebriated soldiers who are guarding him prior to his return to the prison ship. Significantly, the reference occurs during that period of limbo in Israel's life after he has been severed from the beautiful mythic America of his boyhood and immediately before his interminable career as an exile. In trying to escape from the soldiers (the escape that will begin the long chain of events which prohibits his return to America), Israel finds himself in a garden and is able to flee from the soldiers only with the aid of a conveniently located and climbable fruit tree (p. 22). Although the same event occurs in Potter's own narrative,[22] one should keep in mind that Melville omitted innumerable similar details; and, in a book replete with biblical references (for example, Samson among the Philistines), the allusion to Eden seems a deliberate and important one. Israel Potter, after leaving the garden, can never rediscover the earthly utopia. It is worth noting, in light of the book's emphasis on human social relations, that Israel is driven from the garden by two drunken men whose profession is making war.

That Melville developed the symbol of the garden consciously is further indicated by the paragraphs which follow the above-mentioned escape. Israel, alone and a fugitive, rids himself of his handcuffs and is, to some degree, a free man in the natural human world of the English countryside. Impressed by the order and beauty of the scene, he mistakenly thinks that he has stumbled into a park, that is, a serene, protected, garden-like sanctuary. Yet he is soon to learn that this world of man and nature, apparently ordered and safe, is ultimately hostile to his interests. Melville hints at the inimical potential of this world with a slightly clumsy reference to each un-rolling leaf "in very act of escaping from its prison" (p. 22).

It is also notable that Israel's two periods of respite from escaping and being hunted occur when he obtains work as a gardener. He labors first in the garden of the Princess Amelia (p. 36) and then in the King's Gardens at Kew (p. 38). Nonetheless, the periods of sanctuary are brief, and Israel must leave the garden and shift for himself in an unfriendly world. This archetypal symbolism of the garden supports the idea that Melville is dealing with a wider subject than the peculiar fate of a particular man.

Yet, unlike Adam and Eve, Israel Potter does not descend into an unpeopled world. Indeed, Israel's fellow humans are the cause of the two unfortunate patterns that dominate his existence: escape and incarceration. F. O. Matthiessen, in *American Renaissance*, wrote, "As Melville examined man's lot, he was impressed . . . by the terrifying consequences of an individual's separation from his fellow beings."[23] Man needs the company of other men, but human beings are capable of forcing each other into a terrible solitude. An isolated man is a tormented man, and, as Melville points out in *Israel Potter*, isolation need not take the form of physical separation: Israel flees to the city because "crowds are the security . . . the true desert, of persecuted man" (p. 217).[24] Israel's identity as a fugitive is determined by his fear of capture and imprisonment.

The symbolism of captivity, immurement, and enclosure is highly developed in *Israel Potter* and has already been the subject of some critical scrutiny. John T. Frederick[25] accurately points out the connection between the description of New England farm walls in the opening chapter, Israel's semivoluntary incarceration at Squire Woodcock's (Chapter 12), and the brickmaking episodes near the end of the book. Israel's fear of imprisonment represents a dread both of isolation and of death. When faced with the prospect of being "buried alive" in Squire Woodcock's secret chamber, Israel desires, as companions, some flowers and a mirror (p. 95). The flowers are reminiscent of the garden and the pleasure of natural freedom; the sight of his own face in the mirror becomes an affirmation, in prison, of Israel's human identity and a token of his need for companionship.

In one of the few genuinely dramatic passages of *Israel Potter*, Melville, in Chapter 12, captures the full emotional impact of a human being's desperate realization that he is trapped and helpless on earth and that his deliverance may not be forthcoming. Israel's fear of death and the tomb takes complete possession of his being:

It was not the pang of hunger, then, but a nightmare originating in his mysterious incarceration, which appalled him. All through the long hours of this particular night, the sense of being masoned up in the wall, grew and grew, and grew upon him . . . In the blind tomb of the midnight he stretched his two arms sideways, and felt as if coffined at not being able to extend them straight out . . . But still mindful of his promise in this extremity, he uttered no cry. He mutely raved in the darkness. (p. 98)

Squire Woodcock, like Godot, fails to appear, and Israel is rescued from his plight only through his own ingenuity. His resurrection is comic: he slips from his "tomb" to a real funeral chamber and escapes from the house in the clothing of his now-deceased, would-be deliverer. The humor underlines the impossibility of a real incarnation and resurrection from death.

The implications of the pattern of immurement are evident. Solitude, associated with death, is a primitive and basic source of human terror. Man is frequently denied felicity by being "imprisoned" in a variety of ways: by other members of his species and by the existential limitations of his freedom. Israel is also entombed in the pit of the brickyards and finally in the sewers of London. Nor can one forget that Israel is as much a prisoner when he is with Franklin as he is with any one of his innumerable official jailers.[26] The pattern emphasizes the existential fact that man, on earth, is fundamentally *alone*, that he is confined by the very fact of his existence in the world.

This original philosophic solitude is, perhaps, most visible in the example of the common man.

Yet Israel is not always behind bars or walls. Indeed, he very slyly escapes even from Squire Woodcock's. Nevertheless, his condition when he is "free" is very little improved. Circumstances prevent him from seeking human companionship, and, in a variety of similes, poor Israel is compared to a hunted animal.[27] It is unnecessary to enumerate all of the instances in which Israel assumes the role of a fugitive: it should be noted, however, that after pages of rapid description and narration, the first event which Melville describes in detail is Potter's escape from the prison ship (pp. 18–19). Israel, from that point on, is a man pursued, his hunters behind him and a mythic, unattainable goal before him. Confinement in space is only one form of unhappiness—escaping death and isolation does not guarantee protection from other dangers. "Poverty and liberty, or plenty and a prison, seem to be the two horns of the constant dilemma of my life" (p. 96). Political freedom is not existential or economic freedom. Moreover, Israel's condition demands that he distrust other men: he carefully avoids the villages en route to London, and his perceptions become so paranoid that he flees in terror from a poor French bootblack who wants to polish his secret-chamber, message-carrying boots (pp. 50–51). Distrust, as Melville demonstrates in both *Israel Potter* and *The Confidence Man,* is, perhaps, the most significant barrier to man's escape from the torment of social isolation.

In addition to escape and confinement is the motif of changing clothes. At least seven instances of clothes changing are explicitly mentioned by Melville, and each represents, to some extent, a shift in Potter's role, function, or destiny. The first is Israel's assumption of the clothes of an English pauper, and Melville notes that it strangely foreshadows the "long career of destitution before him" (p. 25). This is followed by three outfits that are tokens of relative and temporary prosperity: they are provided by Sir John Millet (p. 35) and by some English friends of the American cause (pp. 45, 49). Events take a turn for the worse, however, and Israel finds himself in the clothing of a dead man (p. 105) and then of a scarecrow (p. 108). Israel's final costume, donned shortly before his arrival in London, is a bundle of rags that, Melville remarks, was probably left on the bank of the pond by some pauper suicide (p. 217). Each time, the clothing calls to mind the desperate reality of Israel's plight: he must assume those identities which are available to him in order to stay alive. Yet it becomes increasingly clear, after his "resurrection" from Squire Woodcock's chamber, that these identities represent a denial of life's rewards and the continuance of an existence that is hardly human.[28]

That Israel's relations to other characters are greatly influenced by the appearance of his clothing is a further commentary upon the role of social status in determining a man's fate.

These three motifs (confinement, escape, and changing clothing) are schematic renderings of the unhappy patterns of a poor man's earthly existence; as such, they are significant elements of the narrative and symbolic structure of *Israel Potter*. They delineate human life as a random series of escapades and actions that form a futile defense against entombment or death. The common man plays a variety of different roles, but never attains to a period of prolonged rest or harmony. Men interact with distrust and hostility and create a complex, ungratifying maze called society. Despite the constant rebuffs, however, Israel never abandons his quest to return to America, to the promised land.

A summary and recapitulation of Israel's chaotic life is given in Chapter 20, entitled "The Shuttle." The section is entirely Melville's invention, and, although it is a relatively minor incident in his hero's history, Melville devotes a full fifteen pages to it. The episode begins when Israel, as the result of his own daring and the enemy's duplicity during a night-time encounter of British and American ships, finds himself alone and unnoticed aboard the enemy ship. Totally helpless, an American among strangers, separated from Paul Jones and his cohorts by an ever-increasing expanse of ocean, Israel must shift for himself to prevent detection and punishment. The causality is entirely implausible, but this, for Melville, is important only insofar as it underlines the equally implausible actions of fate that brought Israel from America to England in the first place. Clearly, the beginning of Chapter 20 is a schematic rendering of the way in which Israel, in a brief period of time, moved from the hospital in Cambridge to the hunted highways of England. As such, it is also a commentary upon the absence of reason and presence of chance in the determination of a man's destiny.

Once on board the British ship, Israel makes a series of valiant but vain attempts to join one of the working crews of the ship (pp. 190–195). He seeks protection in a group identity, but everywhere is treated as an outsider: "Jealous with the spirit of class, no social circle would receive him" (p. 192). At one symbolic level, Israel's encounters with the various crews of the ship represent his attempts, in England, to join different groups of people in order to escape detection as an American. At a more profound level, however, this pattern, in connection with many others in the book, symbolizes man's fundamental desire for social identity and friendly intercourse with other human beings. As such, Israel's failure represents one of the basic ways in which man is thwarted in his search for happiness.

When Israel's bizarre presence on the ship is finally revealed to the entire crew and the officers, Melville evokes the humor of the situation by focusing on the bewilderment of the British sailors. As they gather around Israel, a dialogue ensues that is a paradigm of his existential situation:

". . . Who are you?"
"A poor persecuted fellow at your service, sir."
"Who persecutes you?"
"Every one, sir. All hands seem to be against me."   (p. 197)

This dilemma results in the master-at arms leading Israel back and forth across the ship's deck—which leads to the exchange quoted at the opening of this study:

"To what end do you lead that man about?"
"To no end in the world, sir. I keep leading him about because he has no final destination."   (p. 200)

Both the dialogue and the situation are a commentary upon Israel's life history. Israel escapes detection in this instance, but the lesson is clear. Israel Potter has led a chaotic life, constantly in motion, but with no apparent goal or meaning. Governed by forces beyond his control, forces that, like the master-at-arms, have no ordered plan in which he can play a part, Israel, the common man, shuttles forward and back, with no "final destination."

The patterns of action and circumstance that shape Israel Potter's life after his "fall" from paradise present, symbolically, substantial elements of the conceptual content of the book. As mentioned earlier, *Israel Potter* also contains a number of lengthy historical or social passages that, although interpolated into the plot, are integrated symbolically into Melville's thematic concerns. For the most part, these passages deal with the reality and myth of America.

Israel Potter was originally subtitled "A Fourth of July Story" and is dedicated "To His Highness The Bunker Hill Monument." Strong irony is present from the outset: the celebration day of American independence and the monument to the struggle for independence are both undercut by the example of the Bunker Hill private who fought valiantly and received no reward—not even a much-belated pension from Congress. There is the immediate implication that both the monument and July the Fourth celebrate a victory that is partially hollow if not illusory. These two symbols of America return, together, at the opening of the book's final chapter. The aged Israel Potter, finally achieving his dream of returning to America, lands in Boston on July 4, and narrowly escapes being run over by a "patriotic triumphal car" exhibiting a banner that reads "Bunker Hill, 1775, Glory to the Heroes That Fought" (p. 238). America, intent upon celebrating its myth, ignores its social reality. The riotous crowd virtually tramples a genuine hero for whom America's promises have been and remain unfulfilled.

One of the most important pieces of Melvillian Americana is the treatment of Benjamin Franklin. It is one of three detailed sketches of historical characters and contains one of the few chapters in the book where Israel Potter himself, even briefly, is totally absent from the narrative focus. The chapters devoted to Franklin, however, are not out of harmony with the rest of the text: they provide crucial insights into Melville's account of the causes of Potter's fate.

Franklin is ushered onto the stage with the flourishes of a long, ironically awed description of the "sapient inmate" and his chambers, which reek of antique learning, the "upholstery of science," and buzzing flies (pp. 52–53). Melville's glib pot-shots at Franklin betoken something less than total admiration for one of the Founding Fathers, and the irrelevance to Israel Potter of Franklin's impressive being and surroundings is made clear by the joke of anticlimax: "But when Israel stepped within the chamber, he lost the complete effect of all this; for the sage's back, not his face, was turned to him" (p. 54).

Franklin's further interactions with Israel Potter are important indications of Melville's perceptions about American values and the American way of doing things. Franklin is purportedly a man of virtue and the formulator of a neat system of daily ethics. So we all learned in grade school; so runs the myth. Melville's Franklin is a paternalistic moralist whose ethics reflect an irremediable inability to understand the problems and desires of the common man. His fastidiousness about pecuniary matters and his prohibition of jokes "at funerals or during business transactions" (p. 58) are incomprehensible and distasteful to Israel Potter.

More significant, perhaps, is the way in which Franklin systematically refuses to let Israel be encumbered by any of the pleasures of human life. He denies him wine and pastry and makes an absurd series of arithmetic calculations and arguments to defend that denial. He removes brandy, scented soap, and a delightful young lady from Israel's presence, all the time making sophistic rationalizations of his conduct. These lead to Israel's unforgettable lament that: "Every time he comes in he robs me . . . with an air all the time, too, as if he were making me presents. If he thinks me such a very sensible young man, why not let me take care of myself" (p. 74).

Franklin is a magnificent symbol of what Herbert Marcuse calls "surplus-repression."[29] His ethics, and thus his actions toward Israel, embody the principle of excessive delayed gratification for the sake of some ultimate goal that can only be called "progress." Man's sensual desires are denied, and this denial represents one of the basic sources of man's lack of felicity. Melville's insight is penetrating because the spirit of Franklin ("God helps them that help themselves") is, in fact, a significant component of the spirit of America. Franklin, according to Melville, is "the type and genius of his land" (p. 66). Delayed gratification does build civilizations, but to what end, since it sacrifices many of the members of that civilization? And the habit of thrift quickly becomes the habit of niggardliness. Melville is protesting the kind of rationalism that deprives man of the small, pleasant consolations for his difficult earthly existence.[30] The spirit of self-denial depends upon the assurance of an ultimate reward, and the example of Israel Potter signals the fallaciousness of such an assurance.[31] The spirit of Ben Franklin (the "Protestant ethic") is fundamental to American society: indeed, in Melville's eyes, it is one of the prime reasons that, for the common American man, there is such a

26

marked lack of congruence between the American dream and the American reality.

If, in the psychological topography of *Israel Potter*, Ben Franklin is the super-ego, then Paul Jones is unquestionably the id.[32] Captain Paul, another legendary American hero, seeks a "separate, supreme command" and announces that he lives entirely for the sake of honor and glory (p. 80). Frequently described with similes referring to Indians, Jones "though dressed à-la-mode . . . did not seem to be altogether civilized" (p. 78). It is unnecessary to present a catalogue of his savage virtues: the tattoos beneath Captain Paul's laced coat sleeve are a sufficient emblem of Melville's view of this Revolutionary hero. The description of Captain Paul is an insight into, if not an indictment of, man's capacity to perpetrate evil through violence:

So at midnight, the heart of the metropolis of modern civilization was secretly trod by this jaunty barbarian in broadcloth; a sort of prophetical ghost, glimmering in anticipation upon the advent of those tragic scenes of the French Revolution . . . showing that broaches and finger-rings, not less than nose-rings and tattooing, are tokens of the primeval savageness which ever slumbers in human kind, civilized or uncivilized. (p. 88)

Paul Jones is a symbol not only of an aspect of the external world that affects Israel Potter, but also of a component of Potter's own psyche. A reader cannot ignore the fact that Israel, too, commits his share of violent acts: indeed, he kills more than twenty men in the course of the book. The role of Paul Jones as an internal psychological symbol is made clear when Israel, after disposing of a few British sailors, remarks that "it was Captain Paul's voice that somehow put me up to this deed" (p. 126). Here Melville is closer to Freud than to Rousseau: one of the sources of man's failure lies deeply and unalterably embedded in his own psychological composition.

Chapter 17, one of six chapters dealing more or less directly with Paul Jones, contains a reference that is an important clue to the fictional method of *Israel Potter*. The book is a tribute to the common, forgotten heroes of history, the unknown men who performed essential roles in historical struggles, but received no recompense, not even honor or glory, for their labors. Yet Melville also offers lengthy descriptions of famous men. Does Melville's real interest, then, lie in heroes such as Franklin and Jones? Is Israel being manipulated again, this time as a vehicle for historical portraits? The answer is emphatically "no." Melville is conscious of the seductive appeal of famous heroes, and he converts this appeal into a revealing structural irony. After a lengthy treatment of Captain Paul's exploits and victories, Melville concludes Chapter 17 with the following paragraph: "This cruise made loud fame for

Paul, especially at the court of France, whose king sent Paul a sword and a medal. But poor Israel, who also had conquered a craft, and all unaided too—what had he?" (p. 161). The reader, like historical legend, has focused upon the colorful hero at the expense of the equally heroic cannon-fodder types like Israel: the shift in focus back to the unsung hero, emphasized by the interrogative voice, recapitulates Melville's attempt to call attention to the common, ignored, and much abused American man.

The adventure that epitomizes Paul Jones, of course, is the battle between the *Serapis* and the *Bon Homme Richard*. Melville's description of the battle, although laden with some specimens of execrable writing,[33] is an incisive condemnation of war and of those modern societies for which war is a glorious subject and a common occurrence. Melville eliminates all suspense and drama from his description by revealing the outcome of the battle in the first few paragraphs. The battle is described from an ironic, distant stance, and the reader witnesses a series of absurd, insane, barbaric acts that, according to history, constitute one of the high points in American valor.

There would seem to be something singularly indicatory in this engagement. It may involve at once a type, a parallel, and a prophecy. Sharing the same blood with England, and yet her proved foe in two wars . . . intrepid, unprincipled, reckless, predatory, with boundless ambition, civilized in externals but a savage at heart, America is, or may yet be, the Paul Jones of nations.   (p. 170)

Melville's perceptions are eerily prophetic of the anti-American political critiques of the 1960's. (One cannot forget that Franklin and his style of thinking helped to let Paul Jones loose upon the world.) Melville's desire to glean symbolic content from the battle, however, did not allow him to conclude with politics. The *Serapis-Richard* encounter is a "type" of the violence that men continually direct toward each other: "It seemed more an intestine feud, than a fight between strangers. Or, rather, it was as if the Siamese Twins, oblivious of their fraternal bond, should rage in unnatural fight" (p. 178). The killing is efficient and machine-like: its senselessness is heightened by the reader's knowledge that Paul Jones wages war for reasons of personal vengeance and glory, that idealistic political motives play no part in his thinking. In the end, Melville forcefully undercuts the glory and value of the American victory. "Mutual obliteration from the face of the waters seemed the only natural sequel to hostilities like these. It is, therefore, honor to him as a man, and not reproach to him as an officer, that, to stay such carnage, Captain Pearson, of the Serapis, with his own hands hauled down his colors" (p. 185).

Melville's presentation of the *Serapis-Richard* battle

obviously goes far beyond a denunciation of a specific incident of war. He is saying that war should be an object of revulsion, not of honor, that man's propensity to commit acts of violence is one of the sources of his lack of felicity, that there can be no victory in actions whose aim is the destruction of human life. There is no little significance in the fact that Paul Jones' ship, the *Bon Homme Richard*, is named in explicit honor of the saying that "God helps them that help themselves" (p. 164). Franklin's pithy wisdom also implies that achievement of one's goals means that God is on one's side. In Franklin's terms, Captain Paul and the *Richard* are vindicated, as are any holy crusaders for whom success sanctions both motive and means. With this type of thinking, presumably, the Mexican War and the doctrine of Manifest Destiny are also justified. But what of Israel Potter who has helped himself and received not even a nod from God? The example of his life refutes Franklin's slogan. A nation where "God helps them that help themselves" would indeed be one where an individual's character and actions were given their just reward, yet Melville is asserting that the possibility of such a nation coming into being is jeopardized by man's refusal to obey God's ethical imperatives. (Specifically, one might point to "Love thy neighbor as thyself.") God ought not help man to kill: a nation of violence cannot be just. America, as a violent nation, cannot be the promised land, cannot fulfill its myth. The *Richard,* symbolizing the promise of the myth, sinks out of sight "gorged with slaughter" (p. 186).

One of the few optimistic strains in *Israel Potter* is Melville's presentation of Ethan Allen. Late in the book, as a somewhat inadequate attempt to counterbalance the essentially negative symbolism of Paul Jones and Ben Franklin, Melville introduces a representative of America's potential virtues.

Though born in New England, he exhibited no trace of her character. He was frank, bluff, companionable as a Pagan, convivial as a Roman, hearty as a harvest. His spirit was essentially Western; and herein is his peculiar Americanism; for the Western spirit is, or will yet be (for no other is, or can be) the true American one. (p. 212)

Ethan Allen's assets include honesty, trust, dignity, and a genuine ability to enjoy life's pleasures. He demands humane treatment on earth and expects nothing from the "world of spirits" (p. 207). His "Western spirit," which betrays none of the neuroses of Franklin and Jones, is the only one that can convert America into the real promised land. Yet the West is only a promise, not an actuality. Melville's sketch, unfortunately, is not sufficiently developed to afford many insights into the characteristics of a Melvillian utopia. Ethan Allen, the true American spirit, is seen only when he is a chained captive. He stands in the book as a gleam of potential brightness on Israel Potter's route to Egypt and the City of Dis.

Chapters 23 and 24, jointly entitled "Israel in Egypt" constitute the last of the interpolated scenes to be considered in this analysis. They deal with the inhumane working conditions that accompanied the rise of industrial assembly-line production. Israel, out of desperation, takes a job in a brickyard: this experience furthers his descent toward total poverty and produces in Israel himself a kind of inarticulate nihilism.

Melville's central concern is the effect that labor conditions such as those described or parodied in *Israel Potter* have upon individual men.

Ere entering his pit for the first, Israel had been struck by the dismally devil-may-care gestures of the moulders. But hardly had he himself been a moulder three days, when his previous sedateness of concern at his unfortunate lot, began to conform to the reckless sort of half jolly despair expressed by the others. The truth indeed was, that this continual, violent, helter-skelter slapping of the dough into the moulds, begat a corresponding disposition in the moulder, who, by heedlessly slapping that sad dough . . . was thereby taught, in his meditations, to slap, with similar heedlessness, his own sadder fortunes.   (p. 221)

This type of labor, for Melville, is one of the crucial social evils that keep the common man from the promised land.[34] The worker's life, devoid of pleasure or prosperity, can only lead to a denial of all hope and, indeed, a denial of the value of individual life itself.[35] "What signifies who we be, or where we are, or what we do? . . . All is vanity and clay" (p. 224).

A few pages later, Melville's interest in the existent inequities between economic classes is developed through the almost allegorical treatment of the brick furnaces: "The furnace bricks were haggard, with the immediate blistering of the fire—the midmost ones were ruddy with a genial and tempered glow—the summit ones were pale with the languor of too exclusive an exemption from the burden of the blaze" (p. 224). The technique is overly obvious, but the meaning, at least, is clear. Civilization has many victims, but those who are sacrificed most steadily and most cruelly are the poor, the common men: the Israel Potters for whom America was to be a salvation from tyranny. Industry, in the rising civilizations that Melville observed, had begun to turn men into functional mechanisms. Poverty was intensified by an economic system that forced its victims to work long hours and years without dignity and without hope of escaping the "bondage of Egypt." The progress of civilization is intended to better the lives of its members: the kind of progress that is justified by Franklin and embodied in the brickyard transforms that intention into a grotesque joke.

In *Israel Potter*, Melville's insights into man's social and economic condition are contained in the interplay between the recurrent patterns of action in Israel's adventures and the historical descriptions, which are all interpolations into the *Life and Remarkable Adventures of Israel R. Potter*. These ideas, expressed through a somewhat diagrammatic symbolism, are as relevant to any nineteenth-century "plebian Lear" as they are to Israel Potter. Melville, as Leon Howard has written with reference to *Mardi,* "was asking his boastful countrymen to look beneath the surface of their free institutions and see what these really meant."[36] The life history of Israel Potter is itself an indication that America has failed to meet its promise to be the ideal and just society. Melville's insights reveal that the neglect of Israel Potter was not an accident, that his example is not unique, that the sources of neglect lie deep within the spirit of America and the psyche of man. Moreover, the seeds of the American failure were sown during the period of America's birth: the spirit of Franklin and Jones contributed to America's independence and also to its subsequent maladies.

Israel Potter is not a heap of sketches or a series of loosely connected historical portraits. There exist precise and coherent relationships between its symbolism and its narrative, its solitary hero and its historical sketches.[37]

This is not, of course, to say that *Israel Potter* is a perfectly constructed book. As Charles Feidelson points out,[38] much of the symbolism lacks a functional basis in the narrative, and this defect does a certain damage to the impact of the text. Nevertheless, *Israel Potter* possesses a greater and more subtle unity than has heretofore been ascribed to it. Melville, as usual, was rather tongue in cheek when he wrote to George Putnam that there was "nothing weighty" in *Israel Potter*.[39] What is weighty is guised in episodes rather than rhetoric or pronouncement, and this guise has a peculiar and significant comic ring.

Man is the only animal that laughs and weeps; for he is the only animal that is struck with the difference between what things are, and what they ought to be.

—Hazlitt, "On Wit and Humour"

This critical analysis has so far ignored one of the important elements of the experience of reading *Israel Potter*: humor. *Israel Potter*, in many places, is very funny. Israel's courage and ingenuity offer delightful examples of man's ability to rescue himself from serious plights. The satiric portrait of Franklin enables us to laugh at this pompous and bothersome father-figure. And the descriptions of Israel departing from Squire Woodcock's or fleeing, clad as a scarecrow, through a crowd of bewildered laborers provide instances of frank, almost vaudevillian comedy. Yet ultimately *Israel Potter* is a poignant book. Why, then, the laughter? This chapter is a brief attempt at understanding the function and effects of comedy in this fundamentally serious and gloomy work of fiction.

Among the several different kinds of humor found in *Israel Potter,* satire is the most readily apparent. Melville's satire is directed at the sources of Israel's failure and serves the general purpose of bursting the bubbles of common reputation. Franklin is the most vulnerable satiric object and Melville handles him with an incisive glibness.[40] Paul Jones is similarly treated when his immortal "I have not yet begun to fight" (p. 183), in the context of Melville's description of the *Serapis-Richard* battle, appears as the cry of a deranged barbarian rather than as the courageous assertion of a hero. Melville even slips briefly into satire in his description of the brickyard when he stylistically mimics the repetitive monotony of assembly-line production (p. 220). The satire functions as exposition and enlightens the reader about the real nature of certain sacred American cows.

Israel Potter also contains a number of jokes in which Melville plays language games that have an ultimately serious meaning. One version, of course, is the pun. A typical example is found in the dedication, when Melville refers to Israel Potter as "a private of Bunker Hill, who for his faithful services was years ago promoted to a still deeper privacy under the ground" (p. v). The word play is amusing, but the device also functions as an attack upon the kind of language use that converts dismal realities into pleasing verbal surfaces. A similar and more common technique in *Israel Potter* is one that I can only call "outlandish euphemism." One may take as an example the title of the third chapter: "Israel goes to the wars; and reaching Bunker Hill in time to be of service there, soon after is forced to extend his travels across the sea into the enemy's land." This kind of euphemism is ironic insofar as it calls attention to the fact that it is euphemism. Language can put a pleasing gloss upon reality, but that gloss can be rendered so obvious that the reality itself finally captures the reader's attention. These stylistic devices (in which humor intensifies the reader's awareness) contribute to the general comic tone of *Israel Potter*.

The most bizarre and important kind of comedy in *Israel Potter* is that which takes as its subject the pathetic plight of the faceless hero. This type of humor begins early in the book: for instance, Melville's response to Israel's inability to win his sweetheart in the second chapter is the witty utterance, "The dear, false girl was another's" (p. 13). Or later, with reference to the random vicissitudes of Israel's life, Melville writes: "Thus repeatedly and rapidly were the fortunes of our wanderer planted, torn up, transplanted, and dropped again, hither and thither, according as the Supreme Disposer of sailors and soldiers saw fit to appoint" (p. 119). This comedy, of course, reaches its climax in "The Shuttle," where a fully developed scene serves as a comic symbol of the tragedy of human fate. It is clear that this technique, in part, serves as a buffer against the potential sentimentality of pathos. An ironic voice prevents the book from becoming maudlin. In this particular book, however, such comedy also performs a deeper and more subtle role.

In order to produce this specific type of comedy, Melville's narrative focuses upon acts in themselves, independent of their consequences. In the "scarecrow" scene, for example, Melville describes only the surface appearance of the action and deliberately ignores the effects of the action upon the comic subject, poor Israel Potter. The success of this comedy is contingent upon the facelessness of Israel and the author's refusal to delve into Israel's internal mental apparatus; thus, the reader does not identify with the comic subject. And unquestionably, the appearance of many of Potter's adventures is laughable. There is something undeniably funny about a man, in the garments of a scarecrow, being chased through a field of totally baffled farm workers. There are even strong touches of humor in the nonsensical behavior of the crews of the *Serapis* and the *Richard*. Here too (at least during the early stages of the description), the reader is led to ignore the consequences of this ludicrous scene. Yet the consequences are devastating, and Melville eventually discusses their tragic nature. There is an unresolvable dichotomy in the appearance of human events. The spectacle of men struggling with difficult or insurmountable problems can be a sobering one; but through the reversed telescope of detachment, man and his problems seem quite petty indeed. The comic perspective is one side of Melville's bifurcated view of the human condition. The Melville of *Israel Potter* is part Starbuck and part Stubb, part Ahab and part Ishmael. Man's existential dilemmas are serious ones, yet a pessimistic vision is not totally valid: there *is* humor in the world. One must, from time to time, step back and laugh at one's self and one's world. Pierre's inability to do this is the source of his destruction. Neither the tragic nor the comic stance alone offers a true appraisal of reality: truth, perhaps, exists in the tension between and the coexistence of these two visions.[41]

The dangers of a uniquely comic stance, however, are Melville's primary target in *Israel Potter*. Melville launches a firm attack upon the detached comic perspective that witnesses the plight and ignores the sufferings of the common man. Throughout the first three quarters of the book, the reader is seduced into disengagement from Israel's problems. He enjoys Israel's antics and is mildly thankful that his own fate is more secure and comfortable. Yet one must look at consequences as well as at events. The final chapters of *Israel Potter* are devoid of comedy, and the reader is left gaping at the consequences of Israel's adventures. All of man's skill, courage, and fortitude, embodied in Israel Potter, have proved to be futile weapons against man's social and psychological obstacles. Israel's virtues bring him only poverty and misery. The detached, comic stance, which can celebrate America and ignore Israel Potter, appears to be morally empty.

The light, even whimsical, tone of much of *Israel Potter* would seem more suitable to a tale of man surmounting his obstacles than to a tale of man's total failure. It is as though Fielding's *Joseph Andrews* ended with Joseph in a debtor's prison. The reader, expecting to view the traditional marriage or feast, finds himself staring at "the unupholstered corpse of the beggar" (p. 230). This shift in tone, of course, is deliberate. The comedy was Melville's way of enticing the reader to that pauper's shanty mentioned many pages ago. Melville leads the reader down the path of comic adventures and symbols only to show him the brickyards and gutters at the other end. The reader sees "what is" juxtaposed with "what ought to be." The shift from comedy to pathos heightens the reader's awareness of the reality of suffering and makes him realize that, in "real life" and in literature, comic disengagement alone is "too exclusive an exemption" from the burdens of human existence.

For in this world of lies, Truth is forced to fly like a sacred white doe in the woodlands; and only by cunning glimpses will she reveal herself, as in Shakespeare and other masters of the great Art of Telling the Truth, even though it be covertly and by snatches.

—Melville, "Hawthorne and His Mosses"

The preceding pages of this study represent an attempt to clarify the function and meaning of certain crucial components of Melville's *Israel Potter*. With this accomplished, one may take a few steps back from the text and reflect upon it in light of Melville's theory of fiction and his other work during the 1853–1856 period. This will, I hope, provide a semblance of order for a diverse series of observations about a deceptive and often confusing book.

Allen Hayman, in a discussion of Melville's theory of fiction, correctly concludes that Melville saw the artist as a "searcher after truth."[42] The role of the fiction writer is to perceive and articulate truths about man's social and existential condition. As Melville hints in "Hawthorne and His Mosses," the knowledge of such truths lies more in the domain of the heart and intuition than of the brain and logic.[43] Yet what exactly does Melville mean by that loaded and ambiguous word "truth"? What are the criteria for determining whether or not a given perception is true? Where does one look for truth? How does one recognize it? Although Melville offers no explicit answers to such questions, one may distinguish two basic types of truth in his work. In the realm of social issues, truth resides in the rational and empirical relationship between cause and effect. The writer, as social critic, must perceive this relationship. However, a more compelling species of "truth," for Melville as an artist, is that concerned with man's condition, subjectively perceived. Here, truth is the sum of man's thoughts and feelings about his relationship to the world within and outside him, about the internal and external factors that determine his existential situation. Reality, for a given man, consists not in an object but in the way in which he perceives that object to be related to his desires and hopes. The test of a fictional reality then becomes its ability to correspond with the subjective reality of the reader. The artist who seeks "universal" truth must express those elements of his personal reality which will have some meaning for and relevance to other men.

Moreover, as Melville demonstrates in *Israel Potter* and in great detail in *The Confidence Man,* the appearances of human life are much too deceptive and illusory to be "truth." As Hayman notes, they cannot constitute reality: "A writer concerned with this heightened reality is mainly interested not in the circumstantial events of daily experience, the surface of life, but rather in what lies beneath the surface, the meaning of the surface—the meaning of life, or as much of it as the writer can apprehend."[44] This, of course, is the basis of Melville's distinction between realism and reality: thus, in *The Confidence Man*, Melville asserts that fiction must present "more reality than life itself can show."[45] Or, in a famous citation: "It is with fiction as with religion: it should present another world, and yet one to which we feel the tie."[46]

The patterns and symbols of *Israel Potter* combine to create this other world. The realm of *Israel Potter*, as presented by Melville, is not realism: the causality is too farfetched, the circumstances too implausible. The surface of Israel's life is unique and extraordinary. Yet Melville's fiction captures its more profound reality, with which we all can "feel the tie." The common man has never been through Israel's adventures, but he knows the feeling of being persecuted and the desperate sense of being trapped or "entombed." Neither Melville nor his readers had ever been led back and forth upon the deck of a strange ship, but the feeling of having "no final destination" is a common one. These elements of *Israel Potter* are instantiations of the theory of fiction that Melville would articulate within a year after the completion of his "Fourth of July" story.

Finally one may note Melville's relative lack of concern, in his later work, for the truths of depth psychology, for the determination of precise motivations for human action. There is a link between Israel as a faceless hero and Melville's observations about psychological novels in Chapter 14 of *The Confidence Man*. Although the author refuses to contradict explicitly the psychological novelist's claim that he is unraveling the mysteries of human psychology, he notes that "it may prove suggestive, that all those sallies of ingenuity" have not helped anyone to understand anything.[47] This is not to say that Melville was uninterested in psychology.[48] It is rather to suggest that Melville, in 1855, did not view depth psychology as the primary domain of the novelist. As applied to *Israel Potter,* the statement implies that the novelist's true concern is not the effect of personality upon action, but rather the encroachment of external reality upon any man's (or every man's) search for satisfaction.

This discussion, naturally, leads to a consideration of the particular kind or kinds of truth presented by *Israel Potter*. One type of truth contained in the book, of course, is social. Melville has, in part, sought to portray the causes of civilization's failure to ameliorate the condition of the common man. He has attempted to explain why the reality of America has not matched the myth or promise of America. His insights into the repressive potential of "Franklinism," the pervading horrors of war and violence, and the brutality of new industrial forms are essential components of the "truth" of *Israel Potter*.

The most fundamental truth in the book, however, is the perception that the common man's expectations of happiness are rarely, if ever, fulfilled. This, for Melville, is reality, and he demands that fiction dealing with human fate faithfully mirror that reality. The human failure and unhappiness that partake of this "truth" are Melville's themes in "Bartleby," "The Bell Tower," "Jimmy Rose," "The Happy Failure," "Cock a Doodle Doo," "The Encantadas," the stories of China Aster, Charlemont, the soldier of fortune, and the crippled beggar in *The Confidence Man,* and, of course, *Israel Potter*. "Humanity, thou strong thing, I worship thee, not in the laureled victor but in this vanquished one," wrote Melville in "The Encantadas."[49] According to Melville, the defeat of man's expectations was the most common human destiny: an honestly told story could not violate this truth.

The fact that Israel's fate is shared by innumerable other men is the subject of the final chapters of the book. Here Israel is united with the great dismal crowd of London, that "gulf-stream of humanity" (p. 225) pouring over London Bridge.[50] Chapter 25 evokes a mood of mass apathy and hopelessness, of millions of human beings herded together, alone and unhappy: "Nor marble, nor flesh, nor the sad spirit of man, may in this cindery City of Dis abide white" (p. 227). It is in this context, when the essence, if not the details, of Israel's destiny is shown to be far from unique, that Melville begins to make distinct generalizations about the human condition. "Man, 'poor player,' succeeds better in life's tragedy than comedy" (p. 228). And Israel, "foreknowing, that being of this race, felicity could never be his lot" (p. 228).

Melville's desire to faithfully portray his conception of "reality" is the subject of his few explicit references to the fictional technique of *Israel Potter*. The first of these is found in the dedication:

Well aware that in your Highness' eyes the merit of the story must be in its general fidelity to the main drift of the original narrative, I forbore anywhere to mitigate the hard fortunes of my hero; and . . . durst not substitute for the allotment of Providence any artistic recompense of poetical justice; so that no one can complain of the gloom of my closing chapters more profoundly than myself.   (p. vi)

There is a calculated ambiguity in the phrase "fidelity to the main drift." The fidelity is ostensibly to the general outline of the plot, but in practice it is a fidelity to the implications of a life as unrewarding and unrewarded as that of Israel Potter. Moreover, Melville's refusal to mitigate Israel's fate is a refusal in the name of truth, and truth, for Melville, does not consist in verisimilitude: the relentless misfortunes of Israel Potter are presented not because that is the way they happened in "actuality," but because they correspond to some more profound "reality."

Nonetheless, what was true for Melville may very well not have been attractive to his reading public. Near the end of the book, Melville discusses the literary problems posed by the material of *Israel Potter*:

For just as extreme suffering, without hope, is intolerable to the victim, so, to others, is its depiction without some corresponding delusive mitigation. The gloomiest and truthfulest dramatist seldom chooses for his theme the calamities, however extraordinary, of inferior and private persons; least of all, the pauper's; admonished by the fact, that to the craped palace of the king lying in state, thousands of starers shall throng; but few feel enticed to the shanty, where, like a pealed knuckle-bone, grins the unupholstered corpse of the beggar. (pp. 229–230)

Melville, as we have seen, used the temporary "delusive mitigation" of comedy in order to lure his reader into a view of "extreme suffering, without hope." Yet this passage summons forth two crucial questions about *Israel Potter*. Why did Melville choose as his subject a pauper and not a "king"? And having chosen the pauper, why not genuine tragedy instead of this strange and pessimistic pathos?

The first question may be answered rather simply. Melville was a consciously American writer and in *Israel Potter* he chose to deal with the democratic American hero: the common man.[51] One might also offer a biographical analysis: Melville's personal predicament in 1854 bore much closer similarities to the problems of the masses than to the problems of elevated heroes. That Melville had carried Potter's narrative with him since 1849, however, suggests that his decision to write *Israel Potter* stemmed less from his immediate fiscal and psychological dilemma than from a genuine interest in the meaning of the lives of America's poor and forgotten citizens.

An answer to the second question posed above necessitates a brief examination of some fundamental aspects of tragedy. Tragedy, particularly the Shakespearean tragedy that had an enormous impact upon Melville, is founded upon the possibility of restoring order to the human world. The tragic work climaxes in the death of a hero, but that death is redemptive. Redemption and catharsis are irrevocably intertwined. The hero is sacrificed, but there exists always a character or group of characters who survive and learn from the sacrifice. Thus Fortinbras in *Hamlet* or Edgar and Albany in *King Lear*. Or Ishmael in *Moby Dick*. The tragic hero has been or has become lucid, and his death acquires meaning through his lucidity and the heightened awareness of his survivors. But tragic fate is not the fate of the democratic hero, the common man. He is inarticulate and thus pathetic.[52] His struggles are blind, and his death unnoticed and meaningless. The world of tragedy is not a world to which the common man can "feel the tie." Melville, then, could not write tragedy about the common man because he could not honestly believe that the deaths of such men were meaningful or redemptive, that their sacrifice would restore order to a chaotic world. Indeed, the "tragedy" (in the loose sense of the word) of Israel Potter is precisely the fact that his life and death lacked both meaning and order. Melville's perception of reality would not allow him to mitigate this ultimate misfortune with the "artistic recompense" of genuine tragedy.

The story of China Aster in *The Confidence Man* bears a marked similarity to *Israel Potter*.[53] The candle-maker accepts a friendly loan and, thanks to his unsympathetic beneficiary, lives a life of total poverty and desperation. The story is told as an example, as an illustration of a human ethical principle.[54] In the chapter following the narration of the tale, Frank (the confidence man) and Charlie (Egbert-Thoreau, Winsome-Emerson's disciple) disagree about the lesson to be drawn from it. Charlie believes that it is folly for a friend to help a friend. Frank finds this to be outrageous. The crucial point, of course, is that art, in Melville's eyes, is ultimately moral. The truth which art expresses is a moral truth. Knowledge of reality has ethical implications. The simple narration of a tale, such as Egbert's narration of the story of China Aster, is a narration of appearances, and appearances are deceptive and misleading. The writer of fiction, through various techniques, must elicit the morality from the tale: it is to this end that Melville utilized and developed the story of Israel Potter.

Concluding paragraphs, if they are worth anything, should point to the future rather than back over previous pages. *Israel Potter* has been the victim of critical neglect: I hope some of the neglect has been rectified by this study. A closer and more reflective scrutiny of Melville's work from 1853 to 1856 should provide valuable insights into the mind and environment of the "author of *Moby Dick*," the now renowned writer who was shortly to begin his own thirty years of exile from the realm of fiction. The import of such scrutiny could reach well beyond the arena of scholarship and literary criticism. Melville's perceptions of the American reality and its relationship to the common man have an ominous relevance to the turmoils and crises of the modern world.

WORKS CONSULTED

NOTES

WORKS CONSULTED (*excluding Melville's writings*)

Arvin, Newton. *Herman Melville*. New York, 1950.

Berthoff, Warner. *The Example of Melville*. Princeton, 1962.

Chase, Richard. *Herman Melville*. New York, 1949.

Feidelson, Charles, Jr. *Symbolism and American Literature.* Chicago, 1953.

Frederick, John T. "Symbol and Theme in Melville's *Israel Potter*," *Modern Fiction Studies,* VIII (Autumn 1962), 265–278.

Frye, Northrop. *Anatomy of Criticism*. New York, 1968.

Hayman, Allen. "The Real and the Original: Herman Melville's Theory of Prose Fiction," *Modern Fiction Studies,* VIII (Autumn 1962), 211–235.

Howard, Leon. *Herman Melville*. Berkeley and Los Angeles, 1967.

Leyda, Jay. *The Melville Log*. 2 vols. New York, 1951.

Matthiessen, F. O. *American Renaissance*. London, Toronto, New York, 1941.

McCutcheon, Roger P. "The Technique of Melville's *Israel Potter*," *South Atlantic Quarterly*, XXVII (1928), 161–175.

Miller, Perry. *The Raven and the Whale*. New York, 1956.

Potter, Israel R. *The Life and Remarkable Adventures of Israel R. Potter*. Intro. by Leonard Kriegel. The American Experience Series. New York, 1962.

Rosenberry, Edward H. *Melville and the Comic Spirit*. Cambridge, Mass., 1955.

Sedgwick, William Ellery. *Herman Melville: The Tragedy of Mind*. New York, 1962.

Steiner, George. *The Death of Tragedy*. New York, 1961.

54

NOTES

1. An extensive summary of all critical work on *Israel Potter* through 1962 is contained in an article by John T. Frederick, "Symbol and Theme in Melville's *Israel Potter*," *Modern Fiction Studies*, VIII (Autumn 1962), 265. The list, even supplemented by work done since 1962, is quite brief.

2. Herman Melville, *His Fifty Years of Exile (Israel Potter)* (New York: Sagamore Press, 1957), pp. 229–230. Subsequent page references, to this edition, are included in the text.

3. The following stories, with their dates of publication, reflect these thematic interests: "Bartleby the Scrivener" (November-December 1853), "Cock a Doodle Doo" (December 1853), "The Encantadas" (March-April-May 1854), "Poor Man's Pudding and Rich Man's Crumbs" (June 1854), "The Happy Failure" (July 1854), "The Paradise of Bachelors and The Tartarus of Maids" (April 1855), "The Bell Tower" (submitted in May or June 1855), "Jimmy Rose" (November 1855). *Israel Potter* was published in nine installments from July 1854 through March 1855.

4. Newton Arvin, *Herman Melville* (New York, 1950), p. 251.

5. These terms are derived from the usage of Northrop Frye, *Anatomy of Criticism* (New York, 1968), pp. 38–39. The following excerpts from Frye's discussion of "Tragic Fictional Modes" are especially relevant to *Israel Potter*. "The best word for low mimetic or domestic tragedy is, perhaps, pathos. Pathos presents its hero as isolated by a weakness which appeals to our sympathy because it is on our own level of experience . . .

Pathos is usually concentrated on a single character because low mimetic society is more strongly individualized . . . pathos is increased by the inarticulateness of the victim" (pp. 38–39).

6. The most plausible explanation of the drastic change in Melville's work at this time is offered by Perry Miller in *The Raven and the Whale* (New York, 1956), pp. 307–308. He analyzes the "Young America in Literature" chapter of *Pierre* as Melville's articulation of a conscious break with Evert Duyckinck, Young America, and the idea of a national literature. Up to this point, Melville "had been obliged to learn the terms of his problem from Young America; henceforth he will carry on alone" (p. 308).

7. Warner Berthoff, *The Example of Melville* (Princeton, 1962), p. 15.

8. Leon Howard, *Herman Melville* (Berkeley and Los Angeles, 1967), pp. 213–214.

9. I have only occasionally given significant attention to the sources or the originality of details in Melville's *Israel Potter*. The long scenes that are analyzed are all Melville's inventions. That Melville deliberately included or omitted sections of his source books, that he altered events freely and carefully, has already been established in a lengthy study by Roger P. McCutcheon, "The Technique of Melville's *Israel Potter*," *South Atlantic Quarterly*, XXVII (1928), 161. Melville's persistent habit of supplementing his imagination with source materials is commonly known.

10. Arvin, p. 245.

11. My use, throughout this essay, of the term "existential" requires some explanation. It has nothing explicitly to do with existentialism. By existential problems (crises, issues, etc.) I mean those problems which originate in the fact of a human being's existence in the world, independent of social, economic,

and political factors. "Existential" is thus a less precise version of "ontological." These existential dilemmas, for Melville, seem to be somewhat distinct from the social and economic dilemmas in *Israel Potter*.

12. Herman Melville, *Redburn* (Garden City, N.Y., 1957), p. 290.

13. It is notable that Melville never explained man's unhappiness with exclusively social or exclusively existential arguments. A "social" argument would attribute society's failure to satisfy man to political and economic errors—errors that can be rectified by time, reason, and progress. An "existential" view would hold that man can never attain to complete bliss in any form of civilization and that the expectation of such bliss, however real, is doomed to defeat. These two poles are well symbolized by Rousseau (the social) and the Freud of *Civilization and Its Discontents* (the existential).

14. Howard, p. 124. Chauvinistic American rhetoric is also a recurring subject in Miller's *The Raven and the Whale*.

15. Herman Melville, *White Jacket* (New York, 1956), p. 151.

16. Howard, p. 124.

17. F. O. Matthiessen, *American Renaissance* (London, Toronto, New York, 1941), p. 444.

18. William Ellery Sedgwick, *Herman Melville: The Tragedy of Mind* (New York, 1962), p. 181.

19. Matthiessen, p. 492, observes that for Melville tragedy had become "so real that it could not be written."

20. Howard, p. 214.

21. This distinction is difficult to make because the motifs are sometimes expanded into full-length scenes, e.g., the episode at Squire Woodcock's. Such expansion gives added signif-

icance to the briefer renderings of the motifs. Since my concern is the symbolic content of such events, a precise distinction between brief and elaborate explorations of them is unnecessary.

22. Israel R. Potter, *Life and Remarkable Adventures of Israel R. Potter,* Intro. by Leonard Kriegel, The American Experience Series (New York, 1962), p. 25.

23. Matthiessen, p. 443.

24. The wording of this sentence demands comparison with Melville's introductory description of Benjamin Franklin's rooms in Paris. The walls were hung with "wide maps of far countries in the New World, containing vast empty spaces in the middle, with the word DESERT diffusely printed there" (p. 52).

25. Frederick, pp. 267–270.

26. Indeed, Franklin says to Israel: "You must absolutely remain in your room, just as if you were my prisoner" (p. 59).

27. For example, "the poor panting deer is caught" (p. 29), or a reward for deserters is compared to bounty for "prowling bears" (p. 25).

28. Israel's brief career as a scarecrow, i.e., a mechanical functional man, foreshadows his later occupation as a laborer in the brickyards.

29. Herbert Marcuse, *Eros and Civilization* (New York, 1955), p. 32. Marcuse distinguishes surplus-repression (the restrictions necessitated by social domination) from repression (the modifications of the instincts necessary for the perpetuation of the human race in civilization).

30. Melville's view of the minor sensual pleasures of life is succinctly revealed in a letter to Hawthorne in which he speaks of smuggling a basket of champagne into paradise and re-

marks, "I won't believe in a Temperance Heaven." Jay Leyda, *The Melville Log* (New York, 1951), I, 412–413.

31. The same subject recurs in Chapter 19 of *The Confidence Man*. There, a man who has become a cripple at the hands of the American legal system begins to make sarcastic remarks about "Free Ameriky." The confidence man then delivers a long discourse about the imperfection of human government but, with total optimism, assures the beggar of a "final benignity." Herman Melville, *The Confidence Man* (New York, 1964), p. 104.

32. One might, only semi-facetiously, continue the topography by terming Israel Potter the poor, baffled ego in crisis and Ethan Allen an example of a healthy ego.

33. The foremost example of bad writing in the battle description is Melville's description of the Man-in-the-Moon. "Through this sardonical mist, the face of the Man-in-the-Moon—looking right towards the combatants, as if he were standing in a trap-door of the sea, leaning forward leisurely with his arms complacently folded over upon the edge of the horizon" (p. 175).

34. There is, perhaps, a connection between Melville's decision to develop the descriptions of clay, dust, earth, and bricks in this scene and Israel's surname, "Potter."

35. The relationship between industrialization and the decline of human values is the primary theme of "The Tartarus of Maids." The blatant sexual symbolism in this story establishes a connection between human reproduction and industrial production. For the women who are forced to be a part of the assembly-line, the entire process of human life and reproduction has become a sterile, mechanical one. Melville, again, is concerned with the specific effects of civiliza-

tion upon its members. This theme, obviously, is also present in "Bartleby."

36. Howard, p. 125.

37. Anyone seeking further evidence that *Israel Potter* is a carefully written book should, in light of the themes discussed in the preceding pages, examine closely the opening chapter of the book. There, amidst an ostensibly conventional and serene description of the American countryside, Melville introduces his basic thematic concerns: walls and confinement (p. 3), violence in nature (the crow, p. 4), death and isolation (p. 5), and the notion of anticlimax (in the final paragraph where Israel's ultimate fate is revealed). The anticlimax of the first chapter, moreover, is a paradigm of the anticlimax of Israel's entire life. Given these elements of the opening description, one can sense the full irony of Melville's pronouncement, in the first chapter, that "nor could a fitter country be found for the birthplace of the devoted patriot, Israel Potter" (p. 3).

38. Charles Feidelson, Jr., *Symbolism and American Literature* (Chicago, 1953), p. 183.

39. Cited in Miller, p. 321.

40. The final description of Franklin is a good example of Melville's satire. Franklin stands "as if pondering upon the chance of the important enterprise . . . which, perhaps, might in the sequel affect the weal or woe of nations yet to come." Then he grabs some cork and some feathers from his pocket and proceeds to "whittle away at a shuttlecock of an original scientific construction" (pp. 90–91).

41. Cf. this sentence from the second sketch of "The Encantadas": "Enjoy the bright, keep it turned up perpetually if you can, but be honest and don't deny the black." Melville,

Selected Tales and Poems, ed. Richard Chase (New York, 1966), p. 236.

42. Allen Hayman, "The Real and the Original: Herman Melville's Theory of Prose Fiction," *Modern Fiction Studies,* VIII (Autumn 1962), 211.

43. Herman Melville, "Hawthorne and His Mosses," in *The Shock of Recognition,* ed. Edmund Wilson (New York, 1955), pp. 192–193.

44. Hayman, p. 221.

45. Melville, *The Confidence Man* (New York, 1964), p. 199.

46. *Ibid.*

47. *Ibid.,* p. 73.

48. The description of Paul Jones has important psychological implications, and, of course, depth psychology plays a very important role in *Pierre.*

49. Melville, "The Encantadas," in *Selected Tales and Poems,* ed. Richard Chase (New York, 1966), p. 267.

50. Cf. T. S. Eliot's description of the London Bridge crowd in *The Waste Land,* ll. 60–63.

51. This whole idea, of course, is related to the "Knights and Squires" chapter of *Moby Dick* in which Melville refers to "that democratic dignity which, on all hands, radiates without end from God." In a sense, *Israel Potter* represents another of Melville's attempts to portray the proper American hero. Melville, *Moby Dick,* ed. Charles Feidelson, Jr. (New York, 1964), p. 160.

52. These notions about tragedy relate to the citation from Frye in note 5.

53. "The Story of China Aster" is contained in Chapter 40 of *The Confidence Man.*

54. In a sense, *The Confidence Man* is the structural con-

verse of *Israel Potter*. In the former, exemplary tales are inserts into a general scheme of diagrammatic commentary. In *Israel Potter*, as has been demonstrated, the sections of commentary are inserts into the overall frame of the exemplum.

The LeBaron Russell Briggs Prize
Honors Essays in English

Hawthorne's Conception of the Creative Process
by Richard J. Jacobson • 1965
SBN 674-38275-7

The Natural Work of Art: The Experience of
Romance in Shakespeare's *Winter's Tale*
by John Anthony Williams • 1966
SBN 674-60450-4

Theater as Metaphor in *Hamlet*
by Wendy Coppedge Sanford • 1967
SBN 674-87540-0

The Problem of Shape in *The Prelude:* The Conflict
of Private and Public Speech
by Jonathan R. Grandine • 1968
SBN 674-70800-8

Melville's *Israel Potter:* Reflections on the American
Dream
by Alexander Keyssar • 1969
SBN 674-56475-8

Harvard University Press
Cambridge, Massachusetts